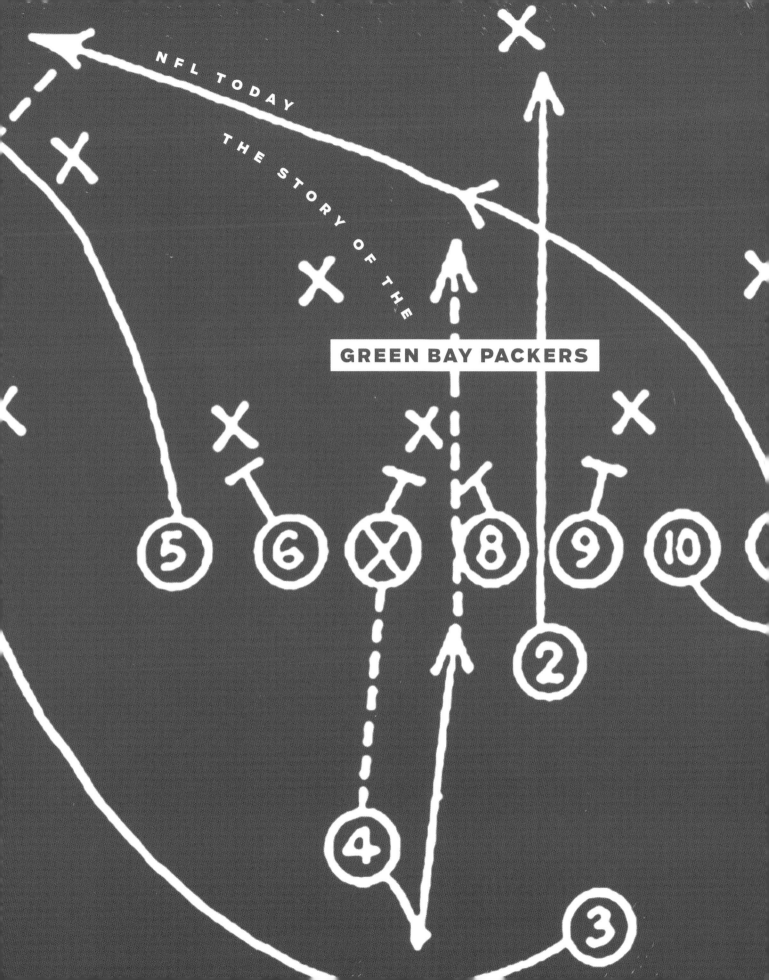

NFL TODAY

THE STORY OF THE

GREEN BAY PACKERS

NFL TODAY

THE STORY OF THE GREEN BAY PACKERS

SARA GILBERT

CREATIVE EDUCATION

PUBLISHED BY CREATIVE EDUCATION
P.O. BOX 227, MANKATO, MINNESOTA 56002
CREATIVE EDUCATION IS AN IMPRINT OF THE CREATIVE COMPANY
WWW.THECREATIVECOMPANY.US

DESIGN AND PRODUCTION BY BLUE DESIGN
ART DIRECTION BY RITA MARSHALL
PRINTED IN THE UNITED STATES OF AMERICA

PHOTOGRAPHS BY AP IMAGES (PRO FOOTBALL HALL
OF FAME), CORBIS (BETTMANN), GETTY IMAGES
(LEE BALTERMAN/SPORTS ILLUSTRATED, JAMES V.
BIEVER, VERNON BIEVER/NFL, MATT CAMPBELL/AFP,
KEVIN CASEY, KEVIN C. COX, TOM DAHLIN, JONATHAN
DANIEL, JONATHAN DANIEL/ALLSPORT, DAVID
DRAPKIN, ELSA, JAMES FLORES/NFL, JEFF GROSS,
AL MESSERSCHMIDT, RONALD C. MODRA/SPORTS
IMAGERY, DARRYL NORENBERG/NFL, PRO FOOTBALL
HALL OF FAME, ART RICKERBY/TIME & LIFE PICTURES,
ROBERT RIGER, FRANK RIPPON/NFL, GREGORY
SHAMUS, DAVID STLUKA, MATTHEW STOCKMAN, JOHN
ZICH/AFP), ROEOMER PHOTOGRAPHY

LIBRARY OF CONGRESS CATALOGING-IN-PUBLICATION DATA
GILBERT, SARA.
THE STORY OF THE GREEN BAY PACKERS / SARA GILBERT.
P. CM. — (NFL TODAY)
INCLUDES INDEX.
SUMMARY: THE HISTORY OF THE NATIONAL FOOTBALL LEAGUE'S
GREEN BAY PACKERS, SURVEYING THE FRANCHISE'S BIGGEST
STARS AND MOST MEMORABLE MOMENTS FROM ITS INAUGURAL
SEASON IN 1919 TO TODAY.
ISBN 978-1-60818-303-6
1. GREEN BAY PACKERS (FOOTBALL TEAM)—HISTORY—JUVENILE
LITERATURE. I. TITLE.

GV956.G7G55 2012
796.332'640977561—DC23   2012031212

9 8 7 6 5 4 3 2

COVER: LINEBACKER CLAY MATTHEWS
PAGE 2: DEFENSIVE BACK WILL BLACKMON
PAGES 4–5: QUARTERBACK BART STARR
PAGE 6: CORNERBACK CHARLES WOODSON

TABLE OF CONTENTS

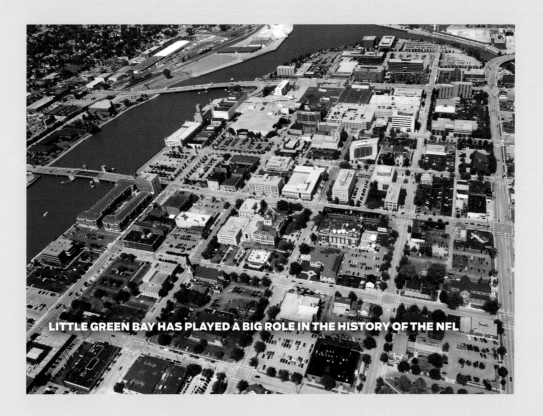

LITTLE GREEN BAY HAS PLAYED A BIG ROLE IN THE HISTORY OF THE NFL

Small Town, Big Team

In 1634, French explorer Jean Nicolet set up a small trading post in the wilderness that later became known as Wisconsin. The local American Indians he encountered there called the arm of Lake Michigan he settled on the "Bay of the Stinking Waters," but Nicolet chose a new name for his post: *La Baie Verte*, which means "the Green Bay." As that settlement evolved into a city that is now home to more than 100,000 people, it maintained the name Nicolet had bestowed upon it, even though the explorer abandoned the fort shortly after building it.

The city of Green Bay has another popular name as well: Titletown. That long-held moniker honors the success of the Green Bay Packers, a National Football League (NFL) team. During their 90-year history in the league, the Packers have brought great notoriety to this small Wisconsin city.

The team got its start in 1919 when a group of local factory workers sat down together in the offices of the Green Bay newspaper to discuss organizing a team.

L–R: EARLY PACKERS RUNNING BACKS ANDY URAM, CLARKE HINKLE, AND ARNIE HERBER

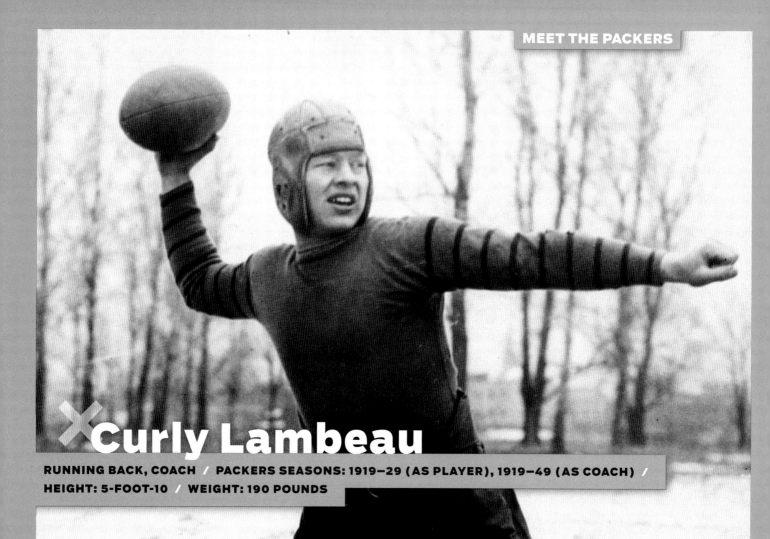

Curly Lambeau

RUNNING BACK, COACH / PACKERS SEASONS: 1919—29 (AS PLAYER), 1919—49 (AS COACH) / HEIGHT: 5-FOOT-10 / WEIGHT: 190 POUNDS

Curly Lambeau was one of the true pioneers of modern professional football, and his place in Green Bay Packers history is legendary. After a standout athletic career at Green Bay East High School, Lambeau enrolled at the University of Notre Dame. But a severe case of tonsillitis soon forced Lambeau to drop out, and before he knew it, he was back in Green Bay, working for the Indian Packing Company, a meat packing business. In 1919, with some financial help from the company for uniforms and a place to practice, Lambeau formed an early version of the football team that would eventually become the Packers. Lambeau starred at halfback and served as coach on early Packers squads that were very successful. He then turned exclusively to coaching, and his innovative ways of utilizing the forward pass changed the game. Throwing the football was rare at the time, but Lambeau's unconventional game plans successfully made passing a viable weapon. He coached the Packers for 31 years in all, and in 1965, the Packers renamed their football stadium "Lambeau Field" in his honor.

CLARKE HINKLE (LEFT) RUSHED FOR 35 SCORES AND BECAME A PACKERS LEGEND

The meeting's leaders, Earl "Curly" Lambeau and George Calhoun, both loved football and wanted to start their own team. After recruiting enough players, the two men asked Lambeau's employer, a meat packing company, to put up $500 for equipment and start-up expenses such as uniforms. To recognize that financial support and the importance of the meat packing industry in Green Bay, the team called itself the Packers.

In 1921, the Packers joined the American Professional Football Association; a year later, that league became the NFL, and the Packers became charter members of the new league. Lambeau was the driving force behind the Packers in the team's early years. For the first 11 seasons, he served as both head coach and running back. A smart and disciplined leader, Lambeau was the first pro coach to implement the forward pass as a major part of his offense. "Curly was always ahead of his time," noted running back Johnny "Blood" McNally, a Packers star of that era. "He was always thinking of ways to get an edge."

"Girls were so amazed by it . . . asking to try it on."

RALPH BRUNO ON HIS CHEESEHEAD HAT CREATION

Sometimes, Lambeau's quest for an advantage got him into trouble, such as the time he recruited two active collegiate players from the University of Notre Dame to play during the 1921 season. The league nearly disenfranchised the team but settled on a $250 fine and an apology from Lambeau instead. Despite Lambeau's usually reliable leadership at the franchise's helm, the Packers often had difficulty making ends meet. Several times, Lambeau sought financial help to keep the team afloat. In 1922, he persuaded a group of local businessmen to purchase the team. They formed the Green Bay Football Corporation, which established the Packers as a team completely owned by the citizens of Green Bay, a unique status that continues to this day.

With his financial problems solved, Lambeau could focus on the business of football. In 1929, he led the Packers to a 12–0–1 record and their first NFL championship. The following season, Lambeau retired as a player and concentrated on coaching. Under his direction and behind the great play of offensive tackle Cal Hubbard and fullback Clarke Hinkle, Green Bay captured two more NFL titles in 1930 and 1931.

In 1933, Green Bay endured the first losing season in its history. But Lambeau soon signed a young end from the University of Alabama named Don Hutson. Sure-handed and blazing fast, Hutson was the NFL's first star receiver. During his 11-year career, he would catch 99 touchdown passes (an NFL record that would stand for 44 years) and lead the league in receptions in 8 seasons. Arnie Herber was most often on the throwing end of such touchdown connections, although he played a wide variety of positions on the field. Largely, though, it was Hutson's brilliant play that propelled the Packers to three more NFL championships in 1936, 1939, and 1944.

After the 1945 season, Hutson retired. Without his heroics, the Packers fell from contention. At the end of the 1949 season, Lambeau stepped down as coach, and Green Bay fell into a losing spiral that would last through much of the 1950s. Quarterback Tobin Rote and receiver Billy Howton had some great seasons in the early 1950s, but the Packers struggled. Three different coaches tried to right the ship after

Cheesy Fashion

In the late 1980s, Chicago White Sox baseball fans began making fun of Milwaukee Brewers fans, calling them "cheeseheads." The term, describing a sports fan from Wisconsin, "The Dairy State," was meant to be an insult, but Brewers fan Ralph Bruno took it as a compliment. He went home, cut a foamy triangle wedge out of his mother's couch cushion, burned black holes in it, painted it yellow, and wore it on his head to a 1987 game. "I don't really remember much that went on during the game because all I could think about was my hat," Bruno said. "Girls were so amazed by it and were asking to try it on." By the end of 1987, Foamation, Inc. of St. Francis, Wisconsin, founded by Bruno, began mass-manufacturing the hats. The hats came in many styles, including the original wedge, a fire hat, a cowboy hat, a crown, and a sombrero. Today, many sports fans associate Cheesehead hats with Packers fans, who can be seen proudly wearing them far and wide, maybe because yellow cheese so beautifully matches the Packers' green and gold colors.

WITH BART STARR AND VINCE LOMBARDI, GREEN BAY RULED THE NFL IN THE '60s

Lambeau's departure, and all three failed. In 1958, the once-proud Packers hit rock bottom, going 1–10–1.

Desperate to turn things around, the Packers then hired a little-known assistant coach from the New York Giants by the name of Vince Lombardi. Lombardi so impressed the hiring committee that he was soon named Green Bay's general manager as well. Lombardi's plan to revive the Packers was based on hard work and discipline, and he intended to stress the physical conditioning of his players. When he assembled the team for the first time in 1959, Lombardi made it clear that things were about to change. "Gentlemen, I've never been part of a losing team," he announced, "and I don't intend to start now."

Don Hutson

END, DEFENSIVE BACK, DEFENSIVE END, KICKER / PACKERS SEASONS: 1935–45 /
HEIGHT: 6-FOOT-1 / WEIGHT: 185 POUNDS

Widely regarded as the first star pass receiver in the NFL, Don Hutson was a speedy jack of all trades on the football field. After Hutson signed contracts on the same day with two teams, the Green Bay Packers and the Brooklyn Dodgers football franchise, NFL president Joe Carr ruled that Hutson should wear a Packers uniform because his Green Bay contract was postmarked 17 minutes before Brooklyn's. Under the tutelage of coach Curly Lambeau, number 14 did it all for the Packers. Hutson caught passes on offense as a receiver, intercepted passes as a defensive back, made tackles as a defensive end, and kicked extra points on special teams. In just one quarter of a game in 1945, Hutson scored an astounding 29 points by catching 4 touchdowns and kicking 5 extra points. For his career, Hutson caught 99 touchdown passes, easily the most ever at the time. He is said to have "invented" many of the passing routes that are run today in the modern game, and he was a relentless worker. "For every pass I caught in a game," Hutson once said, "I caught a thousand in practice."

G Is for Greatness

During Vince Lombardi's third year as the team's head coach in 1961, longtime equipment manager Gerald "Dad" Braisher designed a new logo for the team. His design, a large white *G* placed in a dark green oval, was one of several logos that had been used by the team but the first deemed to be helmet-worthy. Although the popularity of the logo has never been questioned, the actual meaning of the *G* has been debated in recent years. The common assumption has been that the *G* stands for Green Bay, and this may in fact be the case. But legend has it that Coach Lombardi famously motivated his players by telling them that the *G* on their helmets stood for greatness—a claim that was repeated by former NFL player Tiki Barber as he interviewed players prior to the Super Bowl in 2011 and on the team's Wikipedia page. Officially, however, it has never been confirmed. "The Packers have no knowledge of it being anything other than Green Bay," said team spokesman Aaron Popkey. "Maybe it was Tiki Barber having some fun with it."

COACH LOMBARDI HELPED INSTITUTE THE PACKERS' FAMOUS "G" LOGO.

Ticket to Titletown

Timing was on Lombardi's side when he began rebuilding the Packers, as the team already had a core of talented young players in place. Running backs Jim Taylor and Paul Hornung, quarterback Bart Starr, linebacker Ray Nitschke, offensive tackle Forrest Gregg, and defensive backs Willie Wood and Herb Adderley would all eventually be enshrined in the Hall of Fame, but it took Lombardi's demanding coaching style to coax greatness out of them.

In 1960, the young Packers reached the NFL Championship Game but came up short against the Philadelphia Eagles, 17–13. Then, in 1961, they stormed to the NFL title, drubbing the Giants 37–0 in the championship game. The 1962 season was an especially dominant one for the "Pack," as they lost just a single game during the season, a 24–14 contest to the Detroit Lions, and

A MUDDY CLASH BETWEEN THE PACKERS AND CLEVELAND BROWNS IN 1966

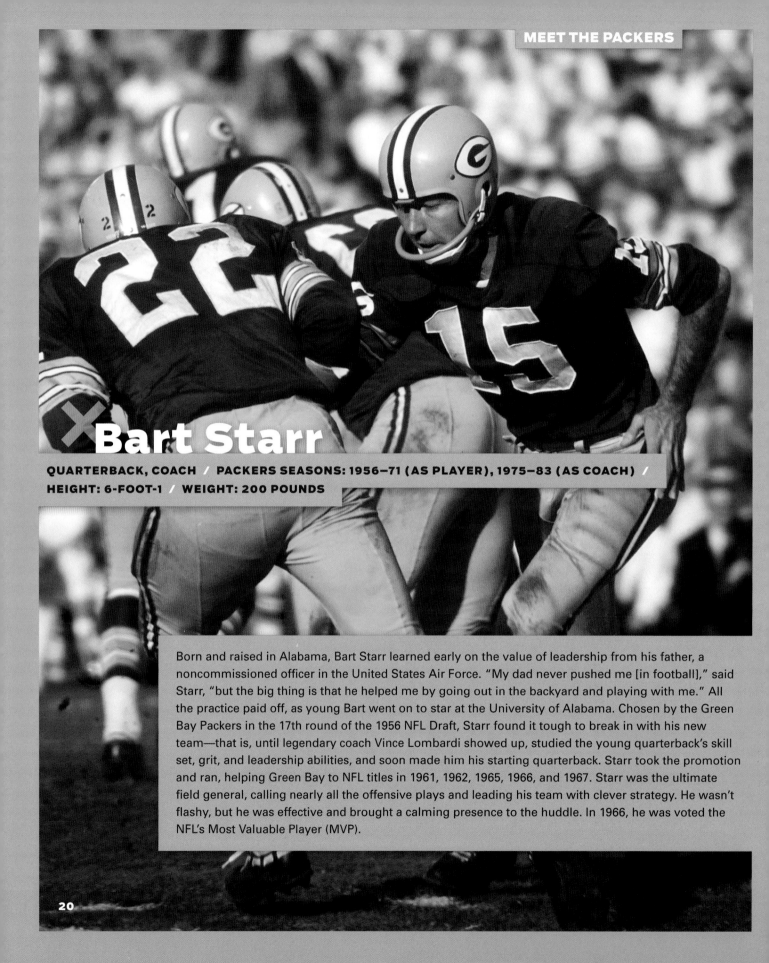

Bart Starr

QUARTERBACK, COACH / PACKERS SEASONS: 1956–71 (AS PLAYER), 1975–83 (AS COACH) /
HEIGHT: 6-FOOT-1 / WEIGHT: 200 POUNDS

Born and raised in Alabama, Bart Starr learned early on the value of leadership from his father, a noncommissioned officer in the United States Air Force. "My dad never pushed me [in football]," said Starr, "but the big thing is that he helped me by going out in the backyard and playing with me." All the practice paid off, as young Bart went on to star at the University of Alabama. Chosen by the Green Bay Packers in the 17th round of the 1956 NFL Draft, Starr found it tough to break in with his new team—that is, until legendary coach Vince Lombardi showed up, studied the young quarterback's skill set, grit, and leadership abilities, and soon made him his starting quarterback. Starr took the promotion and ran, helping Green Bay to NFL titles in 1961, 1962, 1965, 1966, and 1967. Starr was the ultimate field general, calling nearly all the offensive plays and leading his team with clever strategy. He wasn't flashy, but he was effective and brought a calming presence to the huddle. In 1966, he was voted the NFL's Most Valuable Player (MVP).

"It seemed like he never made a mistake."

held their opponents to eight points or fewer an amazing eight times. Defensively, Nitschke, Bill Forester, and Dan Currie led an outstanding linebacking corps, and defensive tackle Henry Jordan anchored the line. In the 1962 NFL Championship Game, the Packers again topped the Giants, this time 16–7. Having watched their team earn eight NFL championships by that point, Packers fans gave their community a new nickname: "Titletown, U.S.A."

While Lombardi was the driving force behind the Packers on the sidelines during those glory years, the players he assembled deserved fair credit. Even with a wealth of stars around him, quarterback Bart Starr was the unmistakable on-field leader of the team. Starr's cool, calm leadership contrasted sharply with Lombardi's loud, fiery style. But while the two men differed in personality, they shared a dedication to perfect execution.

Starr ran the potent Packers offense with the precision of a skilled orchestra conductor, quietly directing his teammates to perform their roles to perfection. With Starr throwing the ball to receiver Carroll Dale and handing it off to Hornung and Taylor, the Packers captured another NFL championship in 1965, defeating the Cleveland Browns 23–12. "Sometimes I wondered if Bart wasn't a machine," Packers guard Jerry Kramer once said. "It seemed like he never made a mistake, never showed any pain, and never missed an open receiver."

Before the 1966 season, the NFL and its rival, the American Football League (AFL), decided to merge. The leagues would keep separate schedules until 1970 but agreed to play a joint championship game starting in 1966. The Packers captured the 1966 NFL title and met the AFL champion Kansas City Chiefs in what was then called the AFL-NFL World Championship Game. Green Bay whipped the Chiefs 35–10 behind two Starr touchdown passes to receiver Max McGee. Shortly thereafter, the game became known by the name it holds today: Super Bowl I. It seemed fitting that the Packers, who had written so much of the NFL's early championship history, should win the very first Super Bowl.

By 1967, Green Bay was an aging team, with many of its stars in their 30s. Despite their advanced

Public Owners

Most major sports teams feature a single prominent owner—generally an older, wealthy individual. In Green Bay, it's hard to describe the team owner, since the franchise has more than 100,000 of them! In a situation unique to the Green Bay Packers, the fans own the team. Since 1923, when Packers founder Curly Lambeau fell into serious debt, the organization has been the property of increasingly larger numbers of stock owners. Packers, Inc., today consists of approximately 4.7 million shares of stock, and no single individual is allowed to possess more than 200,000 shares (which keeps anyone from controlling a majority of the club). In 1997 and 1998, a stock drive increased the number of shares available for purchase, and soon, people from all 50 states, Guam, and the U.S. Virgin Islands became part-owners of the Packers. The drive raised more than $24 million, which went toward refurbishing Lambeau Field. Each year, a meeting of shareholders is held at the stadium, where co-owners occasionally elect a chief executive officer or new board members while discussing the best interests of the team.

HISTORIC LAMBEAU FIELD CAN ACCOMMODATE MORE THAN 73,000 SPECTATORS.

years, the Packers captured another NFL title, this time defeating the Dallas Cowboys in the championship game—a game remembered as one of the most remarkable in NFL history. The game was played at Lambeau Field in Green Bay in such bitterly cold conditions that the contest later became known as the "Ice Bowl."

The temperature that day was -13 degrees, with windchills as low as -48. It was so cold that the turf was like a sheet of ice, and the referees had to end plays by shouting because they were unable to use their whistles, which froze to their lips. Things were not much better for the marching band that was supposed to perform at halftime. Woodwind instruments froze up, brass instruments stuck to lips, and seven members of the band were sent to the hospital with hypothermia. Several of the players involved in the game would complain, years later, of the frostbite they received that fateful afternoon.

With Green Bay trailing 17–14 with 16 seconds left in the game and the Packers on the Cowboys' 1-yard line, Starr called a timeout. After Lombardi told Starr to go for the winning touchdown instead of

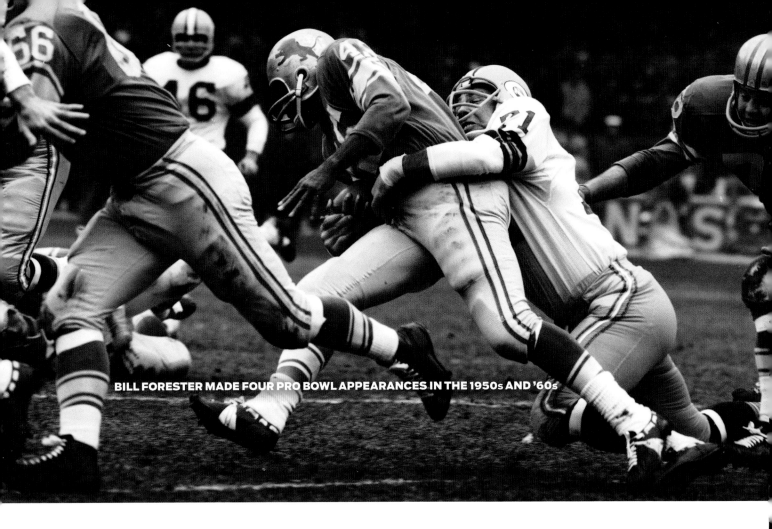

the tying field goal, Starr took the snap and burrowed into the end zone for the championship-clinching score. "That was a game of guts," said Jordan. "Other teams would have quit in that cold. We didn't."

Two weeks later, Green Bay thrashed the Oakland Raiders, 33–14, in Super Bowl II. The lopsided win was historic in several ways. It marked the second time the Packers had won three straight championships, something no other franchise had done even once. The win was also the last for the legendary Lombardi in Green Bay. Exhausted after nine seasons as coach and general manager, Lombardi turned the coaching reins over to his assistant, Phil Bengtson.

In 1968, the Packers missed the playoffs. Shortly after the season, Lombardi left town to take over as coach and general manager of the Washington Redskins. Lombardi's comeback would last only one season, however, before he suddenly died of cancer at the age of 57. To honor him, the NFL named the trophy awarded to the Super Bowl champion the Lombardi Trophy.

The Lambeau Leap

One of the Green Bay Packers' most treasured traditions is the Lambeau Leap. When the home team scores, the Packers player in possession of the ball jumps into the end zone stands to be embraced by adoring Packers fans. The Lambeau Leap began with a spontaneous jump into the Lambeau Field stands by safety LeRoy Butler in 1993 in a game against the Raiders. The leap was preceded by a play in which Butler forced a fumble that was recovered by Packers defensive end Reggie White at the Raiders' 35-yard line. White lateraled the ball to Butler, who ran into the end zone for the touchdown and then made his pioneering leap. The Packers beat the Raiders 28–0 and went on to win a playoff game that season. More than anything, the Lambeau Leap is an expression of the close relationship between Packers players and their fans. And while many other teams have since tried to adopt the leap at their own stadiums, no other team's rapport with its fans has reproduced the same effect as in Green Bay.

THE LAMBEAU LEAP HAS BEEN CELEBRATED IN GREEN BAY FOR 20 YEARS

STERLING SHARPE LED THE LEAGUE IN RECEPTIONS 3 TIMES IN 7 SEASONS

Better Fortunes with Favre

Lombardi's departure marked the end of the Packers' dynasty. Although Packers fans enjoyed great individual performances by such standouts as bruising running back John Brockington, speedy wide receiver James Lofton, and quarterback Don "Majik Man" Majkowski during the 1970s and '80s, victories were hard to come by.

From 1968 to 1991, the Packers posted just five winning seasons. Bringing in players from championship teams past to coach the club didn't help: Bart Starr went 52–76–3 as Green Bay's head coach from 1975 to 1983, and Forrest Gregg went 25–37–1 from 1984 to 1987. Seeking to revive the franchise, the Packers hired Mike Holmgren as head coach in 1992. Holmgren had been an assistant coach with the powerful San Francisco 49ers and had earned a reputation as one of the top offensive strategists in the game. "Mike was a winner, and his attitude rubbed off on us immediately," said brawny receiver Sterling Sharpe, one of the team's brightest stars of the early 1990s and a

BRETT FAVRE INSPIRED TEAMMATES AND FANS WITH HIS ENTHUSIASM FOR THE GAME

Vince Lombardi

COACH / PACKERS SEASONS: 1959–67

"Confidence is contagious. So is lack of confidence." "The only place success comes before work is in the dictionary." "Winning isn't everything—it's the only thing." Vince Lombardi was as quotable as they come. By the time Lombardi began his coaching career, he was prepared, so quotes of wisdom came easily to him. Lombardi was 45 when he became head coach of the Packers in 1959. Before then, he had spent five years earning a solid reputation as an assistant coach with the New York Giants. The Packers were a mess when Lombardi arrived, having won just 1 game in 12 the season before. He told his new team to expect to win right away, and he instilled the same discipline he expected of himself into his team. Sure enough, the Packers finished 7–5 in Lombardi's first season, and in the next eight seasons, they won five championships, including the first two Super Bowls (in 1966 and 1967). Lombardi took up a coaching job with the Redskins in 1969 and turned a 5–9 squad into a 7–5–2 team before succumbing to cancer in 1970. He never had a losing season.

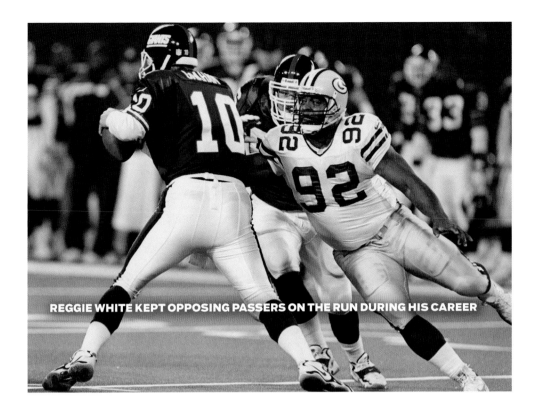

REGGIE WHITE KEPT OPPOSING PASSERS ON THE RUN DURING HIS CAREER

centerpiece of Holmgren's rebuilding plan. "He told us we could be good and rebuilt our pride."

Holmgren was counting on the emergence of young quarterback Brett Favre. Favre had been acquired by the Packers in a trade with the Atlanta Falcons before the 1992 season. The Falcons thought Favre was too raw and undisciplined, but Holmgren saw a promising player with a strong arm and a gift for pulling great plays out of thin air.

Another key step in the Packers' revival was the signing of defensive end Reggie White before the 1993 season. Standing 6-foot-5 and weighing 300 pounds, White was a giant of a man widely recognized as the best defensive lineman in the game. When he arrived in Green Bay, he had already made seven Pro Bowl appearances. The Packers were ready for another run at glory.

Favre and White led Green Bay to playoff appearances in 1993, 1994, and 1995, but each time, the team was thwarted by its old rival: the Dallas Cowboys. In 1996, though, there was no denying the Pack. Favre threw 39 touchdown passes and led Green Bay all the way to the Super Bowl. Facing the New England Patriots for the title, the Packers rode Favre's 2 touchdown passes, White's 3 quarterback sacks, and a crucial 99-yard kick return for a touchdown by Desmond Howard to a 35–21 victory. "It's great to bring a championship back to this town," Favre said. "Our fans deserve this."

The next season, Favre threw 35 touchdown passes and won the NFL MVP award for the third straight year. Green Bay returned to the Super Bowl and was heavily favored to win, but it came up short, losing 31–24 to the Denver Broncos. Following the 1998 season, White retired, and Holmgren left town to become the head coach and general manager of the Seattle Seahawks.

T he Packers remained a contender through the end of the 1990s and into the 21st century, and Favre continued to break one NFL passing record after another. In 1999, he started his 117th consecutive game, breaking the league record for quarterbacks set by the Philadelphia Eagles' Ron Jaworski in 1984. "That tells you a lot about Brett," said Packers wide receiver Antonio Freeman. "He is so competitive and tough, you can't keep him off the field."

Mike Sherman was named the Packers' new head coach in 2000. Sherman recognized that the Packers needed to add some youth to their veteran roster. The new coach began to develop such talented youngsters as explosive running back Ahman Green, wide receiver Donald Driver, defensive tackle Cletidus Hunt, and safety Darren Sharper.

SAFETY LEROY BUTLER (#36) HEADED UP A STINGY DEFENSE IN THE '90s

ANTONIO FREEMAN GAVE BRETT FAVRE A RELIABLE PASSING TARGET FOR EIGHT YEARS

An Iron Streak

It goes without saying that football is a tough game, but quarterback Brett Favre (pictured) took NFL toughness to a new level. Through his 20-year career, he assembled a streak of 297 consecutive games started, easily an NFL record for quarterbacks. The streak started in the fourth week of the 1992 season, Favre's first with the Packers, when starter Don Majkowski was sidelined. Favre led the Packers to a 17–3 win over the Pittsburgh Steelers, and as subsequent wins mounted, he became a fixture. Through the years, he had a total of 18 different Packers backup quarterbacks ready to fill in, and although Favre suffered scores of minor injuries (many resulting from the record 525 sacks he took), the big injury never happened. Some fans considered the consecutive starts streak to be Favre's most impressive statistic, considering the brutal poundings to which NFL quarterbacks are subjected game in and game out. Farve explained the streak with his usual down-to-earth modesty: "There's probably some licks I shouldn't have gotten up from, but maybe some of it is being so stupid and not knowing any different."

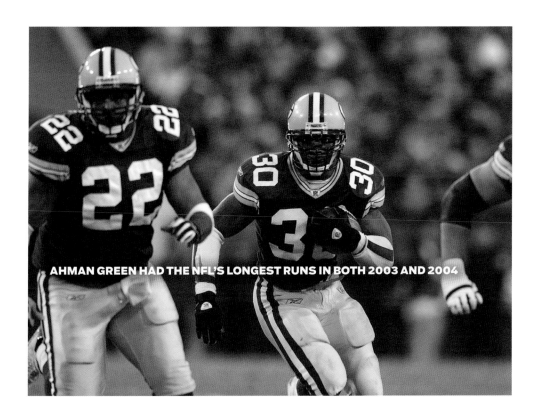

AHMAN GREEN HAD THE NFL'S LONGEST RUNS IN BOTH 2003 AND 2004

In 2001 and 2002, the Packers posted 12–4 records each year but fell in the playoffs. In 2001, they were knocked out of the postseason by the St. Louis Rams. In 2002, Green Bay was stunned by the upstart Atlanta Falcons in the first round of the playoffs, losing 27–7 at Lambeau Field, where it had long enjoyed a terrific home-field advantage during the postseason. "It's a bad end to a great year," said cornerback Mike McKenzie after the loss. "Don't worry about us—we'll be back."

In 2003, the Packers won the new National Football Conference (NFC) North Division with a 10–6 record. Favre put up another impressive season, passing for 32 touchdowns. Green set a number of Packers records, including rushing yards in a single game (218) and a season (1,883), longest run from scrimmage (98 yards), and total number of touchdowns scored in a season (20). The Packers won a wild opening-round playoff game against the Seahawks that was clinched in overtime when Packers cornerback Al Harris returned an interception 52 yards for the winning score in front of a chilled but thrilled Lambeau Field crowd. But the next week, Green Bay lost to the Eagles, 20–17.

Green Bay again captured its division with a 10–6 mark in 2004. The playoffs ended even more bitterly, though, as the rival Minnesota Vikings waltzed into Green Bay, beating the Packers 31–17. That loss seemed to take the fight out of Green Bay, as the Packers slipped to 4–12 in 2005. Favre appeared to have finally lost his touch, throwing a league-leading 29 interceptions and just 20 touchdowns on the season.

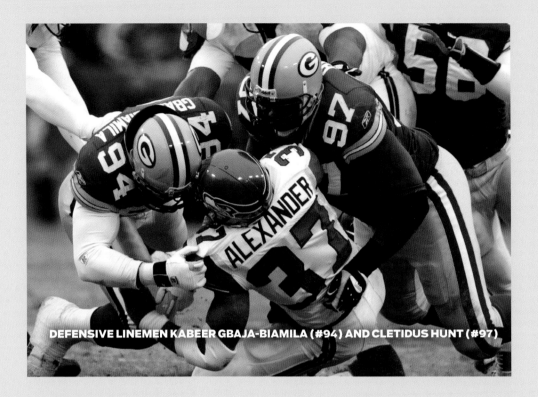

DEFENSIVE LINEMEN KABEER GBAJA-BIAMILA (#94) AND CLETIDUS HUNT (#97)

Lambeau Leaps Again

n 2006, Green Bay hired Mike McCarthy as its new head coach. McCarthy had been the Packers' quarterbacks coach in 1999 and had served as the offensive coordinator for the New Orleans Saints for five years. He had earned a reputation for directing high-scoring offenses and for bringing out the best in the quarterbacks he worked with, and he quickly infused new life into the Packers. Driver caught 92 passes and made the Pro Bowl, as did defensive end Aaron Kampman, who netted 15.5 sacks as the Packers rebounded with an 8–8 record.

McCarthy's attention helped Favre enjoy a renaissance season in 2007. At the age of 38, Favre led the team to a surprising 13–3 record and set several NFL career passing records along the way: all-time completions (5,377), yards (61,655), touchdowns (442), and interceptions (288). Much of Green Bay's success was also due to the development of such youngsters as rookie Ryan Grant, a hard-charging, sure-handed running back out of the University of Notre Dame. Also starring was second-year wide receiver Greg Jennings, who became Favre's favorite target in the end zone, catching 12 touchdowns

RYAN GRANT CHARGED TO A CAREER-BEST 11 TOUCHDOWNS DURING THE 2009 SEASON

Ray Nitschke

LINEBACKER / PACKERS SEASONS: 1958–72 / HEIGHT: 6-FOOT-3 / WEIGHT: 235 POUNDS

If a stranger met Ray Nitschke on the street, Nitschke would have smiled and shaken his hand. If that same stranger met Nitschke on a football field wearing a different-colored uniform, Nitschke would have tried to knock him out. Widely regarded as one of the fiercest tacklers in football history, Nitschke anchored Green Bay's defense throughout the 1960s, a golden era in Packers history. But Nitschke had a hard road to success. Both of his parents died by the time he was 13, so he was raised by his older brothers. After his high school and college days in Illinois, Nitschke played for a 1–10–1 Packers team in his rookie season of 1958, and he didn't know if he fit in. But then new coach Vince Lombardi arrived, the Packers' offense soared, and Nitschke began to shine. From his linebacker position, he crushed ballcarriers with wicked fervor and was athletic enough to intercept 25 passes during his 15-season career. The Packers retired his number 66 jersey in 1983, and he remained a symbol of toughness in Green Bay until he died of a heart attack in 1998.

GREG JENNINGS TOPPED 1,000 RECEIVING YARDS IN 2008, 2009, AND 2010

on the season.

The Packers opened the playoffs with a convincing 42–20 victory over the Seahawks. Then the Giants came to Lambeau for the NFC Championship Game. The contest was a bitterly cold dogfight that was tied at 20 points apiece when time ran out on the clock. Unfortunately, the Packers' magical season ended when, on Green Bay's first overtime possession, Favre threw an interception in Packers territory that led to a game-winning field goal being scored by the Giants.

Shortly after the loss, Favre announced his retirement at a tearful press conference that elicited emotional reactions from football fans in Wisconsin and beyond. He surprised those fans four months later when he

TOUGH RECEIVER DONALD DRIVER WAS A LONGTIME FAN FAVORITE

announced that he had changed his mind and wanted to return. Green Bay, however, shocked the sports world by not immediately welcoming him back. The drama made national headlines for several weeks until the Packers finally announced their decision to move ahead with young quarterback Aaron Rodgers and traded Favre to the New York Jets.

Rodgers, who had served as Favre's backup since 2005, played well in his first season as starter. He helped ease the transition at quarterback by displaying Favre-like intensity under center and throwing for more than 4,000 yards and 28 touchdowns. Despite Rodgers's valiant efforts and the rough-and-tumble tackling of linebacker A. J. Hawk, the 2008 Packers lost their grip on the NFC North crown and fell from the playoff picture.

That turned out to be just a temporary tumble. Athletic tight end Jermichael Finley and crafty cornerback Charles Woodson became fan favorites in Green Bay, and Rodgers, who quickly developed into one of the elite quarterbacks in the league, was soon making those fans almost forget about Favre. The Green Bay faithful demonstrated their allegiance to Rodgers when Favre returned to Lambeau Field with the Minnesota Vikings, who had signed him prior to the 2009 season, in November. The stands echoed with a loud chorus of boos when Favre jogged onto the field before the start of the game, and banners berating Green Bay's one-time hero popped up all over the stadium. Favre and the Vikings beat the Packers 38–26 in that game and added salt to the wound by securing the top spot in the division standings as well. Although the Packers' 11–5 record sent them to the playoffs as the Wild Card team,

Brett Favre

QUARTERBACK / PACKERS SEASONS: 1992–2007 / HEIGHT: 6-FOOT-2 / WEIGHT: 225 POUNDS

Owning most of the NFL's major career passing records, Brett Favre built a storied career. A Mississippi native, Favre was drafted in 1991 by the Atlanta Falcons and spent his rookie year riding the bench. But the Packers traded for him and quickly named him their starting quarterback. After having won just four games in 1991, the 1992 Packers went 9–7, and the 1993 Packers won a first-round playoff game with Favre at the helm. Favre's style of play as a young quarterback was haphazard, owing to his excessive scrambling and tendency to rely on his strong arm to force passes into tight coverage. Occasionally as detrimental to his team as he was helpful, Favre was at least never boring. He showed a knack for leading Green Bay to comeback wins, and by 1996, Favre had led Green Bay to a Super Bowl championship. Number 4 remained a fixture in the lineup until he retired in 2008, tried to return to the team, and was traded to the Jets. He ended his career with the Vikings, retiring after the 2010 season.

CLAY MATTHEWS WAS KNOWN FOR HIS SPEED, PUNISHING HITS, AND LONG HAIR

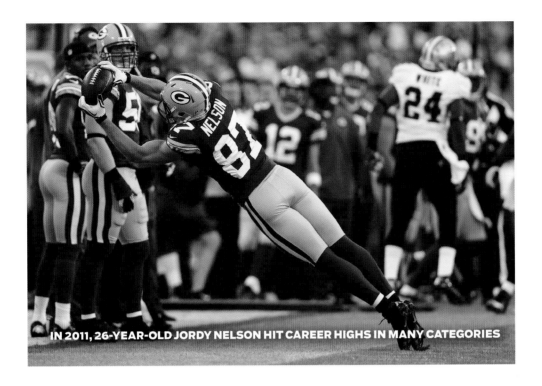

IN 2011, 26-YEAR-OLD JORDY NELSON HIT CAREER HIGHS IN MANY CATEGORIES

they lost a shootout to the Arizona Cardinals, 51–45, in what was the highest-scoring playoff game in NFL history.

Green Bay returned to the postseason (again as the Wild Card team) in 2010. Despite having to play on the road, the Packers won in the first round against the Eagles and in the divisional round against the Atlanta Falcons. That meant they had to face their longtime rivals, the Chicago Bears, in the NFC Championship Game. The Bears had a notoriously stingy defense, but Green Bay managed to score 21 points on its way to a win, which put the Packers back in the Super Bowl. Rodgers was impeccable in his first Super Bowl appearance, throwing three touchdowns and earning the MVP award as the Packers won, 31–25. The award, Coach McCarthy said, was well deserved. "We put everything on his shoulders," he said. "He did a lot at the line of scrimmage for us against a great defense."

Returning the Lombardi Trophy to Titletown brought out the best in the Packers, who started their 2011 campaign with 12 straight wins and ended up with just 1 loss. Rodgers remained the undisputed star, winning the NFL MVP award for his efforts, but running back James Starks and wide receiver Jordy Nelson also played important roles in propelling the Packers back to the playoffs. Third-year linebacker Clay Matthews helped the team throughout the season by pressuring opposing quarterbacks. Unfortunately, hopes of a Super Bowl repeat were dashed by the Giants, who won handily in the divisional round.

Rodgers's Super Belt

Football players have invented many interesting ways to celebrate their successes on the field over the years. Some pound their chests, some point skyward, and some perform a carefully planned dance. At least one was seen pulling out a Sharpie pen and autographing the football with which he had scored. One of the more creative celebrations was started in Green Bay, where quarterback Aaron Rodgers pretended to put a championship belt, like those that boxers and wrestlers wear, around his waist after touchdowns. Although the subtle movement was slow to attract attention, it was being mimicked by opponents, teammates, and fans across the country by the time Rodgers had the opportunity to demonstrate it in Super Bowl XLV. By that time, the movement had become a symbol of the team's offensive strength and a sign of respect among the players. When Rodgers was presented with the Super Bowl MVP award, his teammate, linebacker Clay Matthews, also gave him a gold WWE World Heavyweight Championship belt. "We get excited when we see it," wide receiver Greg Jennings said about Rodgers' celebration. "We know that he's made a play, or we've made a play as an offense."

AS LEADER OF THE HIGH-SCORING PACKERS, AARON RODGERS COULD CELEBRATE OFTEN.

WITH AARON RODGERS AT THE HELM, THE 2012 PACKERS TOOK FIRST IN THE NFC NORTH

BY 2013, THE PACKERS HAD A 74–38 RECORD UNDER COACH MIKE McCARTHY

Expectations for Green Bay's offense were high as the 2012 season began, but after the Packers lost the first game to the 49ers (breaking their streak of 13 regular-season wins at home), doubts began to surface. Despite the shaky start, Rodgers kept the ball moving—especially in Week 6, when he tied the team record for touchdown passes in a game with six. Nelson took three of those passes into the end zone, while wide receiver James Jones picked up two. Jones went on to lead the league in receiving touchdowns with 14 total for the season as the Packers battled back to the top of the NFC North. They stood at 11–5 at season's end, thanks to the rival Vikings' handing them a loss in the final game of regular-season play, but the Packers exacted their revenge one week later in a Wild Card matchup that finished in their favor. Green Bay next met San Francisco in the divisional playoffs and found itself unable to keep up with the 49ers' furtive quarterback, Colin Kaepernick. Following the loss, Packers icon Driver announced his retirement, finishing his 14-season career with team records in receptions and receiving yards, among others.

Although Green Bay is by far the smallest city with an NFL team, it has proven again and again that it can summon big support for its Packers. Fans have filled Lambeau Field for every home game since 1960, a tradition that will no doubt continue in the future as well. And as the Packers continue to bring championships home to Titletown, those fans will continue to cram into the stands of their historic stadium to cheer them on.